Follow the Directions Workbook for Kids

(Preschool, Kindergarten and First Grade)

Kids World Journals and Books

FIND 10 DIFFERENCES

FIND 10 DIFFERENCES

FIND 2
THE SAME
PICTURES

FIND ONE PICTURE WITHOUT A COPY

FIND
ONE
PICTURE
WITHOUT A COPY

FIND ONE PICTURE WITHOUT A COPY

How many pictures do you see? Encircle the number of the correct answer.

6   5   1

6   5   ①

How many pictures do you see? Encircle the number of the correct answer.

3   5   1

How many pictures do you see? Encircle the number of the correct answer.

8   5   9

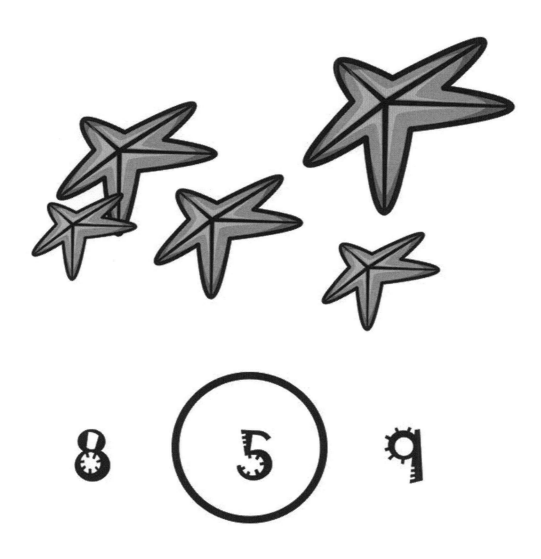

8   (5)   9

How many pictures do you see? Encircle the number of the correct answer.

3   1   7

3   1   7

FIND
ONE
PICTURE
WITHOUT A COPY

FIND
ONE
PICTURE
WITHOUT A COPY

FIND 10 DIFFERENCES

FIND 10 DIFFERENCES

How many pictures do you see? Encircle the number of the correct answer.

6   5   1

6   5   ⑴

Circle 5 dragons.

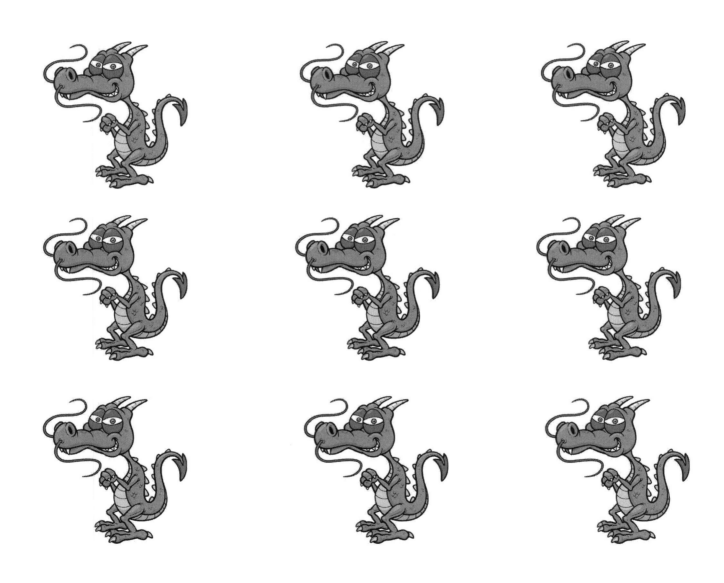

Circle 6 dragons.

Circle 7 pumpkins.

Circle 2 butterflies.

FIND
ONE
PICTURE
WITHOUT A COPY

FIND
ONE
PICTURE
WITHOUT A COPY

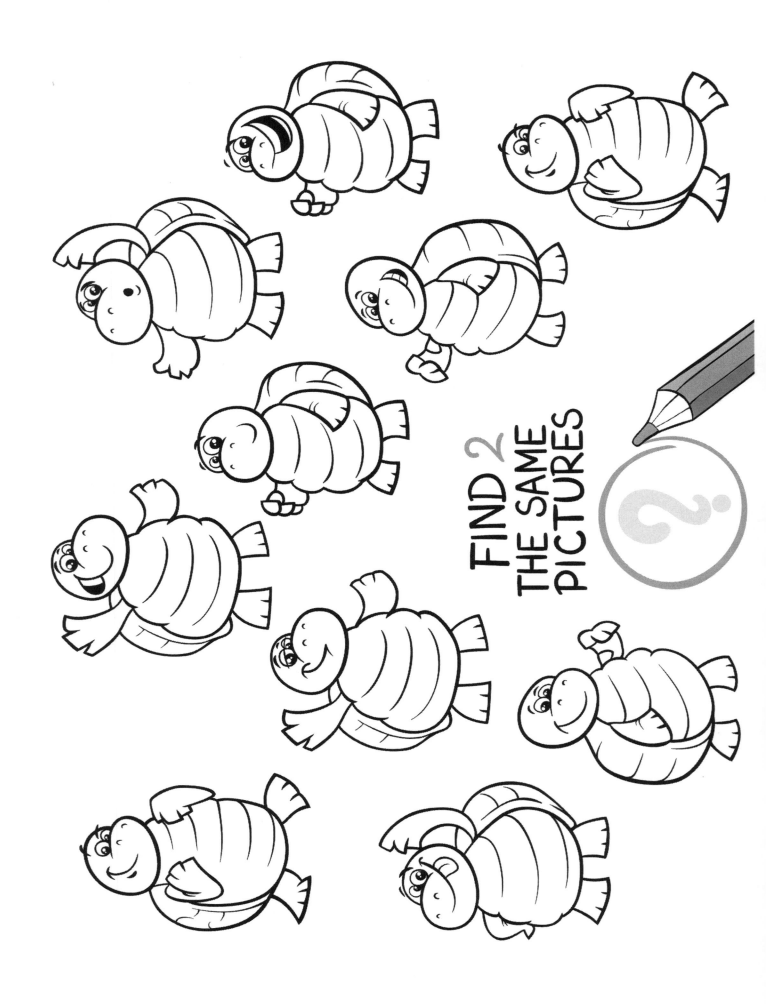

FIND 2
THE SAME PICTURES

FIND 10 DIFFERENCES

FIND 10 DIFFERENCES

FIND 10 DIFFERENCES

FIND 10 DIFFERENCES

How many pictures do you see? Encircle the number of the correct answer.

3   5   1

FIND 10 DIFFERENCES

FIND 2
THE SAME
PICTURES

2.

HOW MANY DOGS DO YOU SEE?

HOW MANY PIGS DO YOU SEE?

HOW MANY CATS
DO YOU SEE?

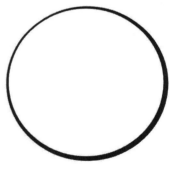

HOW MANY
MONKEYS
DO YOU SEE?

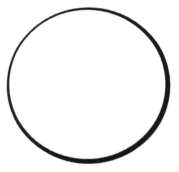

HOW MANY
BIRDS
DO YOU SEE?

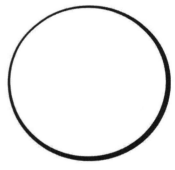

HOW MANY

ELEPHANTS

DO YOU SEE?

Connect each set with the number that goes with it

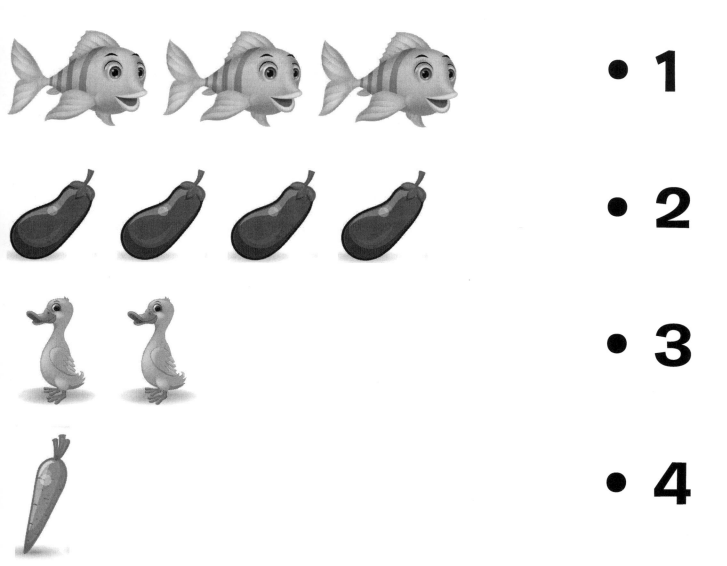

- 1

- 2

- 3

- 4

Write the missing numbers.

Circle the ones that are **different**.

1.

2.

3.

Count the objects and write the number in the box.

1.

2.

3.

Match the object with its word.

- fish

- rabbit

- apple

- orange

Match the object with its word.

- carrot

- bee

- duck

- corn

Match the object with its word.

- pencil

- strawberry

- kite

- ball

Printed in Great Britain
by Amazon